W9-BOD-218

CONGRATULATIONS!
YOU'RE GOING TO BE A
GRANDMOTHER

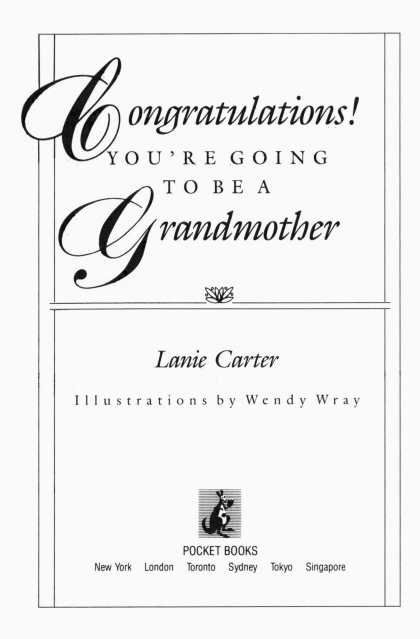

Congratulations!
YOU'RE GOING
TO BE A
Grandmother

Lanie Carter

I l l u s t r a t i o n s   b y   W e n d y   W r a y

POCKET BOOKS

New York   London   Toronto   Sydney   Tokyo   Singapore

The author gratefully acknowledges permission to quote from *What Is a Grandmother?*, by Lee Parr McGrath and Joan Scobey, Essandees Publishers, a division of Simon & Schuster, 1970.

POCKET BOOKS, a division of Simon & Schuster Inc.
1230 Avenue of the Americas, New York, NY 10020

Text copyright © 1980, 1990 by Lanie Carter
Illustrations copyright © 1990 by Wendy Wray

Published by arrangement with the author

All rights reserved, including the right to reproduce this book or portions thereof in any form whatsoever. For information address Pocket Books, 1230 Avenue of the Americas, New York, NY 10020

Carter, Lanie.
    Congratulations! You're going to be a grandmother/Lanie Carter; illustrations by Wendy Wray.
    p.   cm.
    ISBN 0-671-70431-1: $12.95
    1. Grandmothers—United States. 2. Grandparenting—United States.
I. Title.
HQ759.9.C37   1990
306.874'5—dc20   89-77563
                                                  CIP

First Pocket Books hardcover printing May 1990

10   9   8   7   6   5   4   3   2   1

POCKET and colophon are registered trademarks of Simon & Schuster Inc.

Printed in the U.S.A.

Dedicated with Love to
My Grandchildren,
Dayna, Bryan, Brooke, Aron, Kelly, and Freddie
and to the
Many Other Babies
Who Have Touched
My Life

CONTENTS

CONGRATULATIONS!
YOU'RE GOING TO BE A
GRANDMOTHER

Introduction

Dear Grandmother-to-Be,

I came to write this book because . . . well, because I'm the kind of woman who must always have a baby in her arms. Even when I was a child, I could never resist peeking into passing baby carriages.

When I grew up and married, I had my own babies and a husband who was just as child-centered as I am. While we were rearing our own four children, we also were foster parents, and we burped, diapered, patted, and fed babies who needed extra attention while their families were going through difficult times.

After my husband, Bill, passed away and my children left for college or married and moved into homes of their own, there was a great void in my life. I had an empty house, with no husband and no babies, and when a neighborhood physician offered me a job, I jumped at the chance to get out of that empty house and into a busy pediatric office full of squalling infants, worried mothers, and ringing telephones.

Often, when I answered the telephone, I found myself talking to an anxious new mother. Sometimes she only wanted a simple answer to a nonmedical question. "What should I buy for the layette?" said one young woman. Another wanted to know if it was okay to use a regular laundry detergent on her baby's clothes. Some callers just needed reassurance that their babies were doing fine. Young mothers do not automatically know that it is all right for a baby to cry or that hiccups do not signal the beginning of a horrid disease. They also may need to be told that a newborn can sneeze even if he does not have a cold.

Soon, with the blessings of my three "baby doctors," I was giving nonmedical advice to the new mothers. It was the kind of advice that a grandmother might give, and I saw that it filled a need. In our modern, transient world, many young mothers are separated by thousands of miles from their parents, and these young people cannot easily benefit from the childrearing experience of a grandparent's generation.

I researched what new parents needed to know about babies, and in 1974 I started giving classes for expectant parents in the doctors' office. I also started making daily visits to the local hospital to talk to new parents, and my doctors arranged for a twenty-four-hour answering service so that the young mothers and fathers could call me whenever problems arose. Without quite meaning to do it, I had become the world's first professional grandmother.

In 1978 Scripps Memorial Hospital in San Diego gave

me a salary and a classroom so that I could teach pre- and postnatal classes and could easily continue my daily visits to the new families and talk with mothers, fathers, and grandparents. In my years as the New Family Counselor at Scripps, I have grandmothered more than 20,000 babies and have received some 100,000 calls for help on my telephone "warm line."

Frequently I met and talked with grandmothers who had come to help with their son's or daughter's new baby. They almost always had been bright-eyed with anticipation. But too often, I learned later, that same eager grandmother had left days ahead of schedule because of "friction in the household."

The more I heard this, the more it bothered me. I began to ask the new mothers and the new grandmothers what had gone wrong. As I listened to the answers, I became convinced that with some planning, these unhappy situations could and should be avoided.

More and more children today grow up in families in which both parents work. Some children are being raised in single-parent homes. Grandmothers and grandfathers dealing with the changing portrait of today's family may wonder where they fit in. They may struggle to maintain family bonds that not only stretch across continents and oceans, but may include stepgrandchildren, ex-in-laws, step-in-laws, and stepgrandparents.

Yet with this apparently endless upheaval of tradition and traditional roles, there is a need, even a demand, for stability and continuity in family life. Grandparents play such an important part in the lives of their children and grandchildren that they should never abandon the hope of fulfilling that role.

In such a time of family mobility and changing family life-styles, a child needs to learn about his roots, and the grandparents are the roots. If today's nuclear family can

———

become, to a degree, the extended family composed of three generations with all the caring and strength that results from such a unit, our grandchildren can be happier and more secure as they grow up.

For those of you who are just approaching this special time, getting off to a good start is crucial. An important fact to remember is that although babies never change, the life-styles of the parents and methods of childrearing do. Grandparents, especially new ones, may find it difficult not to push the panic button when they discover that their new grandchild is being fed from unsterilized bottles, taking showers with his parents, being given pacifiers, or being wrapped in paper diapers, and yet these newfangled methods all are medically approved.

The first few weeks for new parents are difficult; it is a time of adjustment and working through complex new relationships. Every grandparent's goal should be to offer these new parents reassurance and encouragement—and then, when things settle down, to begin to enjoy his or her new status in the extended family.

Grandchildren, as you will quickly learn, enrich grandparents' lives immeasurably, helping them reach back into the past and dream of the future. Grandchildren help recapture old joys and promise new ones as they grow. Grandparents enhance their grandchildren's lives, too, by helping to reestablish the threatened extended family, providing a sense of tradition, introducing them to a unique aspect of history by telling stories about the past, and showing them understanding and patience.

The emotional attachment between grandparents and grandchildren is unique. The conflicts that occur between parents and children usually do not exist between grandparents and grandchildren. Grandparents and grandchildren are naturally at ease with one another while both have intense emotional relationships with the middle

4

generation. One, grandson, when asked to define a grandparent for Lee Parr McGrath and Joan Scobey's *What Is a Grandmother?*, said that a grandparent is "to spoil you and save you from your parents." Who could ask for a more noble mission in life?

So, it is with much joy that I dedicate this book to grandmothers—lucky people and very special ones.

A Postscript Especially for Grandfathers:

Ten years ago, when I became a professional grandmother, grandfathers were much less active in their grandchildren's lives than they are now. Grandfathers of today can be compared to fathers in this generation: their roles have taken on new importance with respect to the raising of and involvement with the youngsters in their lives. Fathers who "missed out" on the joys of nurturing their own babies because of career pressures are discovering the joys of children for the first time a generation later as grandfathers. And while some grandfathers still have difficulty relating to a leaky bundle of infant, most of them seem to be very much at home as storytellers and companions as their grandchildren grow up.

In essense, although this book is titled *Congratulations! You're Going to Be a Grandmother,* my advice and commentary applies to grandfathers as well. There is little that would make me happier and feel a true sense of accomplishment than to think that this book is being read by grandmothers and grandfathers alike, who together are encouraged to nurture the ties that bind their extended families.

The job of grandparenting rests on all of our shoulders. And the rewards of grandchildren—and healthy families—can be shared by all of us.

New Name, New Role

ARBARA is probably a typical grandmother. She heard about her daughter's pregnancy when her daughter telephoned after her visit to the doctor. While she was happy for her daughter, Barbara later confessed, the news also caused her some dismay.

"You can't kid yourself that you're still young when you're a grandmother," Barbara told me. "When you're a grandmother, you're beginning to get up there."

Even before she told her husband, Barbara called several of her close friends and invited them for coffee. When they arrived, she became flushed and excited. She found herself beginning to make plans and wondered aloud whether she should give a shower for her daughter.

"You don't give the shower when you're the grandmother," said one of her friends. "All you have to do is go to it."

"Oh," said Barbara, and she wondered whether she should be pleased or disappointed. She decided almost immediately that she was pleased. Giving showers was one thing Barbara never truly cared about.

In the weeks that followed, Barbara learned more about the things she would not have to do: She would not have to paint a room for the new baby, or even decide what color the room would be painted. She would not have to stay on a diet or have backaches or throw up in the mornings. She would not have to do breathing exercises, and eventually she would not have to go into a hospital and have the baby.

"I thought at first it was going to be a lot of work," said Barbara. "I don't know why I thought that, except maybe that new little people up until then *had* been a lot of work. It took me a while to catch on, but I did finally figure out that being a grandmother is the fun part! I get to do what I really enjoy, and the part that's a drudge I leave alone."

Barbara went shopping for her grandchild and bought pink things, since she hoped the new baby would be a girl. She also bought a plush doggie that played a tune when it was wound with a key and that was much more expensive than anything she had ever bought for her own children.

The baby was born, and it was a boy, but Barbara did

not even worry about the pink things she had bought. She went right out and got some more in blue. She told me that the baby looked a lot like her husband, and that he had big feet and would probably be tall like his uncle Jack. "Only I think he'll be better looking than Jack," said Barbara. "They're like little miracles, aren't they? Every time one is born, we're getting another chance to go back and do it over—and do it right!"

Barbara's sense of fulfillment upon the birth of her grandchild is shared by most grandparents. The appearance of the new generation is a promise of immortality. The family will go on, and there is no reason why the future should not be even better than the past—why this grandchild should not be the one to reach the goals that were only dreams to his parents and grandparents.

But the hopes are accompanied by anxious shadows of worry. Is the young mother mature enough for her new role? Will the young father be a good parent? What will the world be like when the new grandchild grows up? Will it be a happy place or a bleak, Orwellian desert?

Of course, as a prospective grandmother, you may find yourself wondering and daydreaming long before the baby is born. What kind of grandmother will I be? Will I be a traditional grandmother who reads storybooks and rocks the babies in a chair by the hearth? Will I have the best recipe for gingerbread, and will I knit mittens and kiss away bumps and bruises? Will I be a source of tranquility? A repository of the wisdom of age? Or will I be an exciting "Auntie Mame" sort of grandmother, laughing with her grandchildren and bringing them into a world of delight and sophistication?

Grandfathers, too, will wonder. Will I be a grandfather who is totally immersed in the new baby's every coo and gurgle, or will I feel more comfortable as a storyteller or companion to an older grandchild? Now can be a time for all grandparents to learn the shape and dimensions of the new roles they will play—roles that can be so much more relaxed and easy than the roles of parents, but that have their own limitations and restrictions.

The role of grandparent carries with it one of the most valuable aspects of the family structure, and, therefore, should be strengthened even before the birth of the infant. To accomplish this, parents- and grandparents-to-be need to talk with each other during the pregnancy to discuss expectations and feelings about their new roles.

Just as young couples have to talk to a minister before getting married in a church, parents and grandparents should meet and talk about how much they expect one another to be involved with the child and what kind of impact each hopes to have on the child's life.

Grandparents have a lot to contribute, but how they do so makes all the difference. They have had children of their own, and they speak from direct experience. Although it is sometimes hard for young people to accept because they are not yet feeling confident in their own roles as parents, grandparents are worth listening to—if they speak delicately.

I suggest that these important conversations take place during the pregnancy if possible, because even though it is a most important time, the newborn stage—with its hormonal upheavals and universal fatigue—is not the optimum time for new parents and grandparents to air what may be difficult emotions.

Any grandmother has had many relationships before she approaches this one. You have been a friend, a parent, a wife. The feelings of expectation you experience when you learn that you are going to be a grandmother may be familiar. Something new and exciting is going to happen. But the bond you will share with your grandchild is not like those other bonds—those that bind wife to husband, husband to wife, friend to friend, or parent to child.

The grandmother who is realistic knows that she will

not play the primary role in guiding the development of her grandchild. The parenting will be done by the parents. But the grandparent can touch a child's life in ways that a parent cannot. Grandma and Grandpa can enlarge the child's world and can share with the child a valuable perspective that will enrich his life forever. They can show the child where he is in the plan of things, and they can give the child a sense of permanence and stability. And, of course, they can be a bulwark of strength for the new parents.

As plans are made for the birth of the baby, most young parents realize that they will need help right after the baby is born. Traditionally, it is the maternal grandmother who comes to help out. There is nothing cut and dried about human relationships, however, and sometimes the question of who will help is not easy to answer. The more sensitive the young parents are, the more difficult this decision can be. Whenever this topic comes up, I think of Suzy, who called me when she was in her seventh month of pregnancy.

"We're having a hard time deciding which mother to ask to come stay with me after the baby is born," she said. "We love them both, and we don't want to hurt anyone's feelings."

"Don't you think you'd be more comfortable with your own mother?" I asked her. "After all, you're used to the way she does things."

"Well," said Suzy. That was all she said, and the way she said it should have been a warning. I was newer at my job of professional grandmother then, and I didn't pick up on it.

Suzy went to the hospital and had her baby. When she went home, the maternal grandmother was there, loaded with gifts and glowing with delight. Three days later the maternal grandmother was on a plane home, and Suzy and her husband were making do with the help of a local high school girl who came in every afternoon to make the beds, do the dishes, clean up the kitchen, and help start dinner.

What went wrong?

"I was still my mother's little girl," said Suzy later when she came to see me after she had put the whole incident in perspective. "I hoped that maybe now that I had my own baby, my mother would stop babying me, but she didn't. The second I was home from the hospital, I was being pampered and overprotected just the way I'd been when I was a teen. My mother wouldn't even let me hold the baby for fear he'd spit up on my 'pretty robe.' She did everything for him, and I wasn't learning a thing about taking care of him and being a parent myself.

"Mother wasn't very nice to my husband either. She treated him like the villain of the piece, and she hovered over me and kept talking about how I was supposed to 'recover' from my 'ordeal.' Two more weeks of that and Tom would have been suing for divorce —or maybe I would have. I'm tired now, but at least Tom and I are coping, and it's our baby, and Tom does not have to be a villain, and I do not have to be a victim, and I suppose someday Mom will forgive me."

We can hope so, but after talking with a number of new mothers like Suzy—mothers who experienced difficulties in those first scary days home from the hospital—I began to make a list of dos and don'ts for prospective grandmothers. The list has grown over the years, and from time to time the rules change, but it reads pretty much as follows:

——

It may be difficult
at first to realize your child
is now a parent.

Suzy's case, unfortunately, is typical of many in which the maternal grandmother simply refused to give up her role of mother for the rewarding new one of grandmother. If you are going to have trouble recognizing the fact that your daughter can be a mother—and possibly a very good one—the warning signs probably will appear early in her pregnancy.

Are you sure that she isn't taking proper care of herself? Do you suspect that she doesn't know how to take care of herself? And that her husband doesn't know how to take care of her?

If you must answer yes to any of these questions, watch out—future problems could arise.

Two grandmothers are a double
bonus for the newborn, but probably
not at the same time in
the early weeks.

When Ruth's mother learned that Ruth and Dick were going to be parents, she went immediately to the best department store in town and bought an almost complete layette.

Dick's mother, on the other hand, hurried to her neighborhood knit shop, bought yarn, and soon had made an afghan for the crib. She also made enough receiving blankets to accommodate half the population of Dayton, Ohio, in perfect comfort.

Ruth's mother bought a sterling silver baby mug and a silver photograph frame so that the new arrival could be framed in style once he was photographed.

Dick's mother took the bassinet down from the attic. It was the family bassinet that had been Dick's. She relined it with white satin and then sewed a new skirt for it—eyelet embroidery over satin, with ruffles and bows. Not too practical but done with much love.

The baby arrived, and both grandmothers descended on the young parents, bringing the layettes and the afghans and the sterling silver offerings.

The baby was cooed at and clucked over, and there was a grand competition in the kitchen to see who could bake the tastiest goodies for the new mother and who could heat the nursing bottles to exactly the right temperature. Neither of the grandmothers slept very much because the baby might wake up and need to be changed—which he did, regularly and often.

Ruth spent her first week at home without ever touching the baby except for the time she was actually nursing him. She suffered greatly from feelings of inadequacy, especially since either or both grandmothers were constantly present. If one grandmother wasn't crying "Oh let me!" the other was saying "It's no trouble! I was doing this before you were born!"

After that first week the maternal grandmother went home to tend to her own dusty house and grumpy husband, who had been eating frozen dinners the whole time. The paternal grandmother took a plane back to San Francisco to tend to her job.

———

Ruth and Dick carried the baby home from the airport and immediately knew that they had to change a diaper.

"I did it," said Ruth, "and Dick helped, and when it was done we were both so exhausted that we had to sit down, and Dick had a drink. Then we started to laugh—it was so dumb. We're okay now, but it's a good thing our mothers' visits lasted only a week. If it had gone on much longer, we'd have been paralyzed."

Whenever I hear that both grandmothers are coming to help with the new baby, I do all I can to discourage it. No matter how well the two women get along under normal circumstances, both should not arrive at the same time for an extended stay with the new baby and the young parents. Rivalry will almost surely spring up, and the young parents will be frustrated, uneasy, and probably apprehensive when they should be concentrating on being—and becoming—parents.

And the baby?

Well, any baby who has to entertain two grandmas, both of whom want equal time, is working harder than a baby should when he's so brand new.

If two grandmothers insist on being helpful, I usually suggest that the visits run consecutively. The maternal grandmother usually is there when the new mother first comes home from the hospital. However, there could be many reasons for the paternal grandmother to arrive first. If the grandmothers have worked things out sensibly, one of them stays with the young couple for a week or so. She does not try to make an indelible impression on the new baby, who won't remember anything about the visit anyway. Instead, she does what she can to keep the house running smoothly while the new mother looks after the baby. In due time she leaves the young family to be on its own for a few days. Then, before the young mother can

_____

16

be overwhelmed by the constant demands of the baby, the second grandmother arrives. She is usually welcomed with open arms, and her visit gives the young parents time to get away by themselves for a few hours.

The prospective grandmother
may need to remember that the new
parents are another generation. They may
have a different life-style.

My telephone rang one afternoon and I picked up the receiver to hear sobbing on the other end. It was Renee, who had been in my prenatal class. She had given birth to Jeffrey ten days earlier. He was a fine, healthy baby. She had been happy, and her husband, Bob, had been proud the day the two had taken Jeffrey home. I had received one call from Renee about a diaper rash and then had heard nothing further. Now Renee was on the telephone weeping great tears and hiccuping as she babbled incoherently about somebody's mother.

It took Renee a few minutes to calm down. Then she told me what the trouble was—and the trouble was with her mother.

"She came the day we got home from the hospital," said Renee, "and she doesn't approve of me! My own mother doesn't approve of me! She says I'm spoiled and selfish. She says Bob is a terrible father. He just took her to the airport. I don't think she'll ever speak to me again! I don't know how I could have done such a thing!"

As it turned out, what Renee had done was to play some music on the stereo. Actually, she had played rather a lot of music on the stereo, since both she and Bob were rock music fans. Renee and Bob had not embarked on their home music festival without proper forethought. When they had talked to the pediatrician during their prenatal visit, they had asked if the music would bother the baby.

"I'm going to take it for granted that you aren't talking about music that's turned up to a volume that makes the walls vibrate," said the pediatrician. "No fair shattering the baby's eardrums. But if it's not too loud, the music definitely won't hurt a thing. A newborn should get used to the regular household noises—vacuum cleaners, barking dogs, and music too. It isn't necessary to tiptoe around just because you've got a baby in the house."

So Renee and Bob had played their music. And what had Renee's mother done when she arrived? She had tiptoed. She had shushed Bob and Renee, and she had strongly indicated that visitors should talk in whispers. Needless to say, she had taken strong exception to the music that the young parents both loved.

Although Jeffrey was a good baby, he did cry now and then. Whenever he cried, Grandma would say, "No wonder! That crazy music is upsetting him!"

"We tried to cool it," said Renee. "We figured Mother wasn't going to stay very long, and we could play the stereo later, when she left. Then Bob brought home a new tape and we wanted to try it, and when Jeffrey woke up from his nap, he started to cry."

"He wanted to let you know he was awake," I told Renee.

"Well, sure," said Renee. "He always cries when he wakes up. But Mother marched into the room and she said, 'That music goes or I go!' Well, we'd been trying so hard, and we both got mad. I saw Bob turn red, like he was going to choke. And before I could think about it, I said, 'Okay. You go.'"

It was unfortunate. It should not have happened. If the new grandmother had taken up her role with a live-and-let-live attitude, it would not have happened.

Bear in mind that you do not necessarily have two strikes on you if the new mother is a daughter-in-law.

Sometimes it is the paternal grandmother who lives nearby or who has the time to give when the new baby comes home. In my experience, mothers-in-law are far more loved and accepted than one would believe after hearing all the jokes. In many cases, the mother-in-law and the young wife are close friends. Sometimes the young wife feels intimidated by her own mother and will turn to her mother-in-law when she has problems.

If you have not already established a good rapport with your daughter-in-law, the advent of your first grandchild will be an ideal time to begin. But examine your own attitudes with scrupulous honesty. When there is a problem with the in-law relationship, it usually arises from jealousy. Have you been overprotective of your son? Do you feel that his new wife is not really good enough for him? Deep down in your heart, do you object to sharing his love with this young woman—this outsider?

If you detect even a trace of these attitudes in yourself, get busy. Look for things to like about your daughter-in-law. Even if she does not do things quite the way you do, keep an open mind. There are probably rituals and customs she learned from her mother with which she is comfortable. You may be wiser and happier if you respect them. Remember that we are never too old to learn new things.

Sometimes there are conflicts in families, and they cannot be resolved. If this is the case, it would be madness to try to help the young mother when she brings the baby home. Other arrangements will have to be made, but do try to keep the lines of communication open. If you are not able to be friends, there is no need to be enemies. You do not want to lose contact with your grandchild, who will always be a part of your family—and an extension of yourself.

*Of course you are going to love
your new grandchild. Babies are easy to love.
But give first consideration to the
new mother.*

"My mother was the perfect grandmother," Cindy told me. "I took care of the baby, and she ran the support system. She did the shopping and the cooking and she kept the house going. She also made me feel pretty special. It even beats cooking to have somebody with you who's warm and affectionate and supportive."

That pretty well sums up what you are planning to do, and if you can do it without upsetting the household or forcing your ways onto the young couple, so much the better.

Be flexible.

If you have no other demands on your time—and the expectant parents agree—you may decide to arrive a week or so before the baby is due. You will have a chance to visit, to help with the last-minute preparations, and to get the feel of the household.

If this is not a practical idea, you may want to set things up so that you can arrive after labor has begun or after the baby has been born. Keep in mind the fact that very few babies arrive on the day they are due. Sometimes they come weeks ahead of time. Often they are late. More than one prospective grandmother has arrived on the date the baby was due and then had to leave before the birth, or before the baby came home from the hospital, to get back to a job.

Whether the baby is early or late, and whether you are a person with unlimited time or a busy career woman, it is the attitude you will bring to your new role as a grandparent that will set the stage for a lifetime of family sharing. Three generations—parents, children, and grandparents—all have their unique gifts to contribute. As time passes, the relationships and interactions in the new family system will change, and that is as it should be. With a good start, the chances are that the changes will be healthy ones and that the family will grow ever stronger.

The More Things Change, the More They Stay the Same

E V E N though it may have been years since you have handled a baby, chances are that you are not going to feel strange with your newborn grandchild in your arms. Babies still cry, sneeze, have hiccups, spit up, and wet with great regularity. If they are healthy, not much is apt to go wrong. Babies are tolerant and permissive, moreover, and will not even notice if the new grandmother who picks them up is a bit clumsy, or if she does not diaper them correctly.

Of course, handling a baby is a knack, and if you are relaxed, you soon will "have it" again, just as you once had it when your own children were small. You will help the new mother relax too.

But if babies do not change, childrearing methods do. To avoid shock, bewilderment, and outrage, you may want to bring yourself up-to-date on the new ways before you risk an argument with the new parents.

For example:

Germs are no longer terribly scary.

Today's grandmother has vivid memories of hours spent sterilizing bottles and nipples. You may remember the fear that the nipple would be contaminated by handling as you tried to put it onto the bottle. Today it is hard to explain what the big worry was all about. Babies are not that fragile, and even the most tenderly cared for child has come into contact with billions of germs by the time he is a few hours old.

Do not give vent to any little screams of fright and horror when you see your newborn grandchild being fed cold milk from a nursing bottle that has just been taken from the refrigerator. It is all right! Most pediatricians approve.

Most pediatricians also agree that the nursing bottle need not be sterilized. Nowadays hot sudsy water is all that is needed to wash nursing bottles. After they are washed, they are rinsed well, or put through a cycle in the dishwasher. The formula goes in after the dishwasher has completed its performance. The bottles go into the refrigerator, and the new mother is all set.

Disposable diapers are just as respectable as the other kind.

The very first time I was asked to baby-sit with my new grandchild, her parents arrived with a box of disposable diapers. I was horrified. I was sure that a "good" mother always used cloth diapers. I said as much. The new parents left, taking the baby, and the disposable diapers, with them.

It was one of my bigger mistakes. I was stubborn about it too. I wanted to prove my point, and I wanted to make sure my grandchild was being treated properly. So I did a study of babies who were diapered with disposables and compared them with babies who were diapered with cloth.

There was no difference between the two groups of babies. Paper absorbs as well as cloth, and babies are notoriously indifferent about what is wrapped around their bottoms. The parents probably will decide about disposable versus cloth depending on their life-styles and attitudes, and there is no need for the new grandmother even to comment on their decision.

Pacifiers will not disfigure a child for life, nor are they likely to destroy his character.

25

When we were bringing up our children, pacifiers were taboo. It was widely believed that a baby who was permitted to suck on a pacifier would end up with a malformed mouth. Pacifiers also were supposed to lead to infections, since once the baby began to suck on one, it could not be kept sterile.

Today the thinking about pacifiers has changed. Some pediatricians still disapprove of them, but most feel that babies need extra sucking. "If we don't allow a baby a pacifier," says one pediatrician, "he may find his thumb. Thumb-sucking can lead to malformations of the jaw. Also, when the sucking instinct diminishes at about six months of age, it is not difficult to take a pacifier away from the baby. It is impossible to take away his thumb."

To use a pacifier or not to use one is a choice that new parents will make with their baby's doctor. Like the choice between disposable diapers and cloth, it should pass without comment from the grandmother.

Unless they are actually going to journey to the Arctic, babies do not need to be bundled too warmly.

With my first grandchild I made the mistake of overbundling. I was keeping the baby overnight for the first time, and I was in a frenzy of carefulness. I had kept a nice woolen baby blanket down through the years, and I saw to it that the baby was swaddled securely in it so that no stray draft could chill her. I also saw to it that the room where she slept was nice and warm.

The baby wakened in the night, crying, and I found her bathed in perspiration from head to foot.

I changed her and held her, and when she went back to sleep, I covered her with a lighter blanket. When the new parents came for her the next day, I casually asked whether they kept her room nice and warm when they put her down to sleep.

"No," said the young mother, "not especially. She gets along the way we do—with the room at the same temperature as ours. The pediatrician says it isn't good to keep her room too warm or to overbundle her. The books all say the same thing."

Many baby products have changed since we had our children.

To this day, even though I always have my grandchildren buckled safely in a car seat, my arm flies to the passenger side when I come to a quick stop—that was our safety device for a generation and more ago. Thank heavens car seats are now mandatory.

Strollers are made to be transported easily to accommodate new parents' active life-styles. Umbrella strollers and lightweight folding strollers are much handier for parents than the old cumbersome carriages, and even if they look flimsy to you, you need not worry as I did about their giving adequate support to the baby's back. All the doctors I have worked with assured me that they're fine. The latest rage is a running stroller for athletic moms and dads so baby can share outdoor fun.

The front-pack carrier is another innovation. When this

is used, the baby is carried comfortably in front of its parent or grandparent. Infants thrive on the warmth as they cuddle against the person who is "wearing" them. These carriers can be used from birth until they graduate to backpacks, about six months of age.

Cribs and bassinets are not necessarily the same these days. More and more parents are buying water mattresses for the baby's crib, and the old-fashioned wicker bassinet is giving way to a wonderful, clear-sided bassinet called the "C-Baby." This was designed so the infant can be watched and admired at all times, and to give the parents and grandparents the peace of mind that all is well. This unit comes with optional water mattress that has proven an effective calming device for fussy babies, a wonderful gift from grandparents.

Another useful gift might be an automatic swing. This can be a godsend for the young parents after the grandmother leaves. The infant sits comfortably in the seat while the swing gently moves back and forth, keeping the baby happy and amused.

Babies do not need solids right away.

When our children were born, there often was competition among the new mothers about the variety of solid foods their babies could consume.

"Johnny had cereal at three weeks," one young mother might say.

The young mother would then be topped by a friend who started her infant on vegetables at two weeks. The really gifted baby ate more solids earlier than the other newborns in the neighborhood. There was something virtuous about persuading a tiny baby to eat applesauce. It was on a par with entering him in Harvard the day he was born.

Today most pediatricians suggest that mothers put off giving their babies solid food for four to six months. There are two reasons for this: First, a baby will get all the nourishment his body needs from the milk he is taking. Second, pediatricians believe that if solids are offered too early, there is a greater chance that the baby will develop problems with allergies.

In the matter of nourishment, be guided by the new mother, who is surely being guided by the pediatrician. And never, never tell the new parents that the baby wouldn't cry so much if he were getting enough to eat!

Any mention of food immediately brings us to the subject of breast-feeding. This is an area of child care in which there is great conflict between new parents and grandmothers.

When we had our children, formula feeding was almost the rule. Those of us who did breast-feed enjoyed two advantages: We stayed in the hospital longer, since breast milk generally comes in on the third or fourth day. Then, when we went home, our milk and feeding schedules were established—and once we were at home we had the support of mothers and grandmothers who had successfully breast-fed.

Many new mothers today leave the hospital before their milk is in. A schedule is hard to establish during the first days home, so the poor mother seems to be nursing all the time. Also, breasts are not like bottles. It is hard for the nursing mother to be sure how much milk her baby is getting. With breast-feeding, as with most other areas of child care, the mother and the grandmother need to be relaxed. Anxiety is the big enemy. It may be difficult for the grandmother to hear her new grandchild crying, and even more difficult for her to keep from telling the mother that she does not have enough milk.

Remember that only a very small percentage of healthy mothers cannot breast-feed. All the mother needs if she is to be successful is encouragement—lots of it! Bring her plenty of fluids (ten to twelve glasses a day), make sure she is eating a balanced diet, reassure her and love her, and you will have a healthy, well-nourished grandchild.

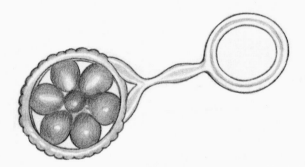

A bath is a bath is a bath.

Not much has changed since you bathed your own babies, except that today more and more fathers are getting into the sudsy water up to their elbows, and frequently parents are showering with their babies.

New parents are more flexible today about how often the baby is bathed and about the time of the bath. It need not necessarily be in the morning. Child care is more casual now and often more comfortable. Many fathers have attended prenatal classes and learned how to care for their babies. However, most young men still harbor a secret fear that the baby will break if he is not held correctly, and they are delighted to have a grandmother on hand for reassurance during the first few baths.

In helping bathe the baby, as in everything you do for the young parents, reassurance is the key word. You are there to encourage, not to take over. In time, the young couple will be on their own with the baby. It will be your main concern to help them get there easily and soon.

Most new moms resume their careers.

Diapers, pacifiers, and sterilizing bottles all are minor issues that grandmothers may want to know about before their new grandchild arrives. However, in my contact with most grandparents, their biggest concern revolves around the new mother's return to the workforce.

Unlike in our day, most new moms do choose to return to their jobs, either because they want to or because of economic necessity. When my daughter made her decision to become a full-time student after her first child was born, it was very hard for me to accept this. In fact, I did not have good feelings about her choice at all, believing, as many women in my generation do, that mothers should stay at home with their children, at least for the first few years of the children's lives. Not only is the mother the best person to care for the child, but the thought of leaving a tiny baby in someone else's care sent shivers down my spine.

Now that I have witnessed several grandchildren survive day care and preschool, I can reassure you that most of the time children do just fine by this option. In some ways, because most neighborhoods have changed since we were young and no longer offer natural peer groups for children (and young mothers), day care and preschool provide an opportunity for children to learn to play with others, an experience that they cannot get at home.

The bottom line is that as a grandmother, you really have no choice but to accept the new parents' decision. If you do otherwise and tell your daughter she should not return to work, you will only cause additional friction in the family. Your children undoubtedly made their choice after a lot of thinking about their financial situation and consideration of their child-rearing philosophy. Your disapproval will undermine their decision and is likely to place additional guilt on the new mother especially, who you can be certain already is having a hard time coping with the pull and tug of career versus full-time motherhood.

If you wish to influence your grandchild's care and you are willing to pitch in and help, you can offer to watch the child part-time, if you live close by. Ideally, you could be there if the child or parent is sick and needs special attention. Or you could pick up the child early from day care one day a week, as I do with one of my grandchildren. Not only does this routine give my daughter a few hours to herself after work, but it gives me a special time with my granddaughter, which she and I both look forward to every week.

Your reaction to whatever decision your children make about child care should be equally tolerant, even if it is the husband who is the one to stay home and the wife to return to an office. In the cases I know like this, the fathers are able to pursue their careers while at home, and the mothers report equal fulfillment on the job.

The most important lesson to remember is that no matter what decision they make, the new parents will struggle with its pros and cons and will need extra reassurance during the period of adjustment when working any amount of time is tearing them away from the new child they love very much. It is the grandparents' job to be supportive. In the end, the new family will find its own balance.

THREE

The New Family

T the beginning of this century, almost all babies were born at home. Then, in the years between 1910 and 1920, women began to go to hospitals to give birth. The hospital was considered the safest place for both the mother and the child. It still is.

With the majority of births taking place in hospitals, the mortality rate dropped dramatically. However, there were many things about the hospital experience that were depressing and even dehumanizing.

Many young mothers in the forties, fifties, and sixties felt that they ceased to be people when they were subjected to the hospital routine. They were no longer surrounded by family. Since it was not "sterile" to have anyone other than hospital personnel in the labor room or the delivery room, even the husbands could not be there to encourage and support the mothers. When she was actually about to give birth, the mother was sedated so completely that she was really not present when her child first appeared in the world.

She recovered consciousness after it was all over. Usually she was back in her room, and the nurse was bringing in the new baby—wrapped and swaddled and red-faced with outrage—so that the mother could have a peek at him and be assured that she had indeed had a child.

In this arrangement, fathers were tolerated to a certain degree. They were informed when the baby was safely born and they were told the sex of the child. After the birth they were allowed to visit the mother at designated hours. They were almost never allowed to hold the baby. Instead, they looked at the child through the glass window of the nursery.

The mother stayed in the hospital for a week or more, and the baby was brought into her room to be fed every four hours. When it was time for the mother to go home, her child was still a stranger.

Clinically, the iron routine of the maternity ward was fine. Psychologically, it was all wrong. In time we learned that expectant mothers need the support of loved ones during labor and delivery. Husbands want to feel needed

---

during this important time. And babies need to bond with their parents.

A bond is something that binds things together, that unites individuals into a group. The word *bonding* became very popular during the sixties and seventies to describe something that took place easily and naturally when the birth occurred at home. It is the process by which the child becomes a part of the family and learns to recognize the parents who nourish him and care for him. The child also becomes part of a group that can include grandparents, aunts, uncles, and siblings.

Until recently, however, the baby who was born in a hospital setting had very little chance to know the people who would be most important in his life. His contact with his mother was fragmentary, and his father did not even exist for him until he was a week old. Siblings, grandparents, and other family members did not appear on the scene at all.

Gradually the family, the doctors, and the nurses came to realize that the traditional hospital routine needed to be changed. The old hard-line, inflexible routine of the maternity ward was eased, so today parents-to-be share the whole birth experience. The mother-to-be is not deposited in a labor room by herself. Instead, the father-to-be is with her, helping time the contractions, comforting, and encouraging.

When the birth is imminent, the mother is not nearly as sedated as she would have been twenty years ago. Sometimes, if she has had childbirth classes and has done her breathing exercises, she is not sedated at all. She is not an inert object during the birth. She is working and cooperating, and she sees her baby the moment it is born. She holds the child even before the umbilical cord is cut, and if the father is in the delivery room (as he usually is), he holds the baby too. Bonding begins to take place.

The newborn is often amazingly alert during the first hour after birth, and good eye contact takes place. Usually the baby goes into a deep sleep after that first hour. He may sleep for eight to sixteen hours, and the mother has a chance to rest.

Rooming-in is available in most hospitals today. When the new family chooses rooming-in, the baby stays with the mother. Mother, father, and baby have a chance to be together during much of the hospital stay. The rigid four-hour feeding schedules have been abolished, and the newborns are fed on reasonable demand.

In some hospitals the extended family, and not just the parents, share in the birth experience. It might not be practical to have uncles, aunts, siblings, cousins, and mothers-in-law present in the delivery room. However, parents who want the warmth and support of other family members can elect to use a facility in some hospitals called the alternative birth center, or the LDR (labor-delivery-recovery) room.

The alternative birth center (ABC), or LDR, looks like an ordinary bedroom in an ordinary home. It contains a bed that does not resemble a hospital bed, comfortable chairs for several people, and usually a television set. Sometimes the mother who plans to give birth in this room takes special classes to teach her to cope with labor and delivery without medication. Then, when it is time for her baby to arrive, she is not put into a labor room, moved to a delivery room, and then moved into a recovery room. Instead, she stays in the bed, just as she would stay in her own bed if she were giving birth at home. Family members and friends may witness the birth and share the joy with the new family. In an alternative birth center or LDR, the grandmother can be part of the experience if she desires! And if the parents are willing.

Whether you witness the birth or not, you will have to recognize the fact that when that baby arrives into the world, your child has become a parent. Nothing will ever be the same. It may help to think back to the first time you became a parent and to remember the many important changes that occurred in your life and your husband's. It was a time of great adjustment for you; it will be the same for your child. Perhaps the new mother and father will be a bit frightened and uncertain. If so, the new grandmother can give them encouragement and praise, helping them feel comfortable in their new roles.

The grandmother who is wise will try to do this without making the young people feel inadequate. They are probably going to feel slightly inadequate at first in any event, but if the grandmother tries to take over—to show how well she can change a diaper or burp the baby—the young mother may respond with the resentment a child feels toward an overbearing mother. If you plan to be a truly beloved grandmother, it is important to realize that your help is greatly needed—and that it must be tempered with wisdom and moderation.

Again, a few suggestions may guide you in helping the new family in the best way.

First, before you define your role, talk things over with the other members of the cast.

———

If you can, spend some time chatting with the young parents before the baby comes. Find out about areas in which you can be most helpful.

Your primary goal probably will be to keep the household running smoothly while the young parents become better acquainted with the baby. Although today's grandmother is frequently a career woman, she can bring her own brand of creativity to this task.

Creativity does not imply rearranging the living room furniture or painting the second bathroom. The less uproar at this time the better. The new parents have plenty of changes with which to cope without having their surroundings tampered with. But the new grandmother may want to cook special dishes and serve them attractively. She may think of delightful ways to make the new mother feel treasured and appreciated.

"I really missed my mom after she left," Wendy told me. "The first few days I was home from the hospital, she would make my bed up fresh while I took my shower, and she'd always have a clean nightgown ready for me. We kept the baby with us in our room, and every night my mother made up a 'night pack' for us. There was a change of clothes in it, and diapers and disposable washcloths. I didn't even have to get out of bed to change the baby when she woke up for feeding."

A "night pack" is a marvelous idea. And what new mother will not appreciate a special comfortable corner where she can feed the baby? This can be arranged with a rocking chair, if one is available, or simply a chair that the mother will find comfortable as she sits with the baby in her arms. There should be a soft light, a table to hold a glass of juice or milk if the mother is nursing, and a nursing bottle if she is not. Do not forget the cloth the mother will need when she burps the baby.

You might suggest that you be the one to answer the telephone while the new mother is resting, or while she is feeding the baby. Have a pad and pencil handy to take messages.

You might ask if there is any ironing to do. Even in this age of wash-and-wear clothes, most households have a small heap of ironing hidden away in a drawer or on a closet shelf. The young mother might be glad to know that this is being taken care of.

Are you an expert needlewoman? You might ask about mending that needs to be done, or hems that could be taken up or let down. Now that the baby is on the scene clamoring for attention, the young mother will not have much time for this sort of task.

Is baking your forté? What could be nicer or more cozy for new parents than to cuddle with the baby as the aroma of homemade cookies wafts from the kitchen?

I am sure most grandmothers will think of many other nice things to do. Go to it, but do check with the new parents before you undertake anything that could be considered a reorganization.

*If the young parents seem
afraid of the baby, or harried,
or even resentful,
do not be upset.*

Parental love may not spring forth at the moment of birth. Sometimes it takes a while. Babies are very small and often, when they are very new, unattractive.

"Bill looked like a monkey!" said one young mother.

"I worked like a horse to get him born, and that's the way he paid me back. Red in the face, too, and he yelled thirty-two hours a day."

"Long day," I said.

"You'd better believe it," said the young mother.

Most young women are not this forthright. If they are disappointed in their babies, or if they do not experience a warm rush of maternal feeling when they hold their newborns, they may become quiet. They may withdraw and brood. These mothers are not "unnatural." The maternal feelings will come. Perhaps the young mother will not feel the blissful ecstasy that one reads about in books and on greeting cards, but the young mother will love her baby, and the child who looks like a monkey (or a tadpole—lots of babies resemble tadpoles) will shape up, lose his magenta tint, and eventually grow hair. It just takes a little while.

Paternal emotions may be even longer in asserting themselves. The new father has not actually given birth. He is usually gone all day, and he may not feel that the new little human being on the scene is real, or that the baby is now a permanent part of his life. Give daddy a little space, and he will come around too.

Even if you are looking after the household, you do not need to be there nonstop.

Keep your sensitivity working; you may get the message now and then that the new family needs to be alone for a little while.

Feelings of rejection are neither becoming nor appropriate at this point. It does not matter if you have traveled across the country to be with your daughter. It does not matter if you have slogged through snowdrifts to get to the hospital. If the new mother and daddy want to be alone with their baby—or just with each other—respect their privacy.

If there is a dog, you might want to take him for a walk. If there is no dog, offer to do some marketing. You can always pick up some favorite fruit juices that will be important for the nursing mother.

Things can be even easier at Grandma's house.

If grandparents live close enough and there is room for the new family, the young parents and the newborn may go to the grandparents' house for the first week or so after they leave the hospital. This arrangement can work out very well.

When the young people are guests in your home, it is easier and more natural for you to assume the kitchen duties. Since you know where things are, you do not need to worry about upsetting someone else's arrangements as you go about preparing meals and looking after the house. Also, you will sleep better in your bed, and thus will be more rested when you deal with the daytime chores. The new mother also may rest better when she does not have to concern herself with what is going on in the household.

The new grandparent who is helping to care for the baby in her own home has one temptation, however. She may want to show off the grandchild to friends. Remember that the fewer people the new parents have to see in the first week or so, the better. They are both weary. Just take this time to get to know your new pride and joy. After a few weeks everyone will be ready to meet the public.

Regardless of who is visiting whom, remember that you will be a guest in the home of your daughter or daughter-in-law—or she will be a guest in your home.

Plan to show the young parents the same courtesy you would show a stranger. The first days home from the hospital can be a time of sharing, learning, and serenity rather than an ordeal to be survived.

An example from my own life may shed some light on the ways in which a new grandma has to bend to accommodate her children's needs and wishes.

When my oldest grandchild was born, I was fortunate enough to have my daughter and son-in-law come and spend the first few days home from the hospital at my house. I had fixed up a room for the parents and the baby, and I cannot tell you how special it was to have my baby granddaughter and her mommy taking a nap in the afternoon, with me in the kitchen fixing a dinner that I knew the whole family would enjoy. It was a very cozy and warm feeling, and I had a great sense of well-being.

After a grandchild is born, most grandparents share that warm feeling simply because they do worry before the birth that everything is going to go well. That sense of well-being is probably strongest once the child is home from the hospital and under its own roof, or even better, its grandparents' roof!

Four months after my first grandchild was born, one of my other daughters had her first boy. Her husband had decided to take that week off, and when they said that they were going to stay home and be together, of course my feelings were hurt. My children lived so close by, and I had thought I could just go over early in the morning and fix their meals. I wanted to feel needed.

With their plans I was not quite sure whether I should call them the next day. If I did not hear from them in a week, should I worry or should I call? I did not want to interfere.

All was resolved, however, when the next morning after my daughter arrived home from the hospital, she called me—in tears. The baby had been up all night, and she was sure they had been doing everything wrong. And she said, "Mom, would you come over and help?"

Of course, I was in my car in an instant. I went over and everything was fine, she just needed a little help. Her husband, who had not been around babies much, was not sure if what they were doing was right. On the third or fourth night my daughter asked me to spend the night, and from then on I just continued to be available at her request.

So we got through the first week, as did my eldest daughter and I, each experience totally different, but in both cases, off to a good grandparenting start.

Enjoy yourself, and don't be afraid of touching.

Two of the saddest people I have ever known are Charles and Jonathan, who were born to a registered nurse during that bleak period in our history when babies were not supposed to be touched. In addition to being a firm believer in nontouching, Margaret, their mother, was terrified of germs. Her boys were hygienically raised. They were not cuddled, since cuddling would spoil the boys and would lead to an unhealthy exchange of germs between mother and child.

Everything with which the boys came into contact was kept sterile until they were a year old. Even after that there was very little of the normal give-and-take that happens with youngsters. Charles never got a lick of Jonathan's lollipop, and Jonathan did not drink out of Charles's glass.

The boys were fed on a schedule as strict as that in any hospital. They were not picked up when they cried, but were left to "cry it out."

When they were older—but not too old—they were given a thorough grounding in the facts of life. One suspects that this hygienic approach carried over into this part of their education. Their mother explained the entire matter in terms of fish and farm animals, taking them on several visits to model dairies and at least one pig farm. She explained that sex was perfectly normal and natural and that all creatures did it, and of course she hoped that they would not become curious and take to experimenting when they reached their teens and possibly get into trouble.

The boys grew, flourished, were chock full of vitamins, had straight teeth, and exercised regularly. They did not get into trouble with sex in their teens, possibly because too much hygiene can take the romance out of anything.

Charles became a tennis instructor and now holds forth in Phoenix and has been unable to form a lasting attachment with any woman. He sees his mother once every year or two. She cannot understand how he can neglect her so. She took such good care of him when he was small.

Jonathan married, had one child, then found the closeness of the connubial bond almost suffocating. There were no more children, and Jonathan now lives in an apartment over the garage. He has his own television set there, a photographic darkroom, and a fine collection of tapes and records.

The moral is clear. In this case, total sterility can lead to a life of total sterility. Touching is a good thing. The more a baby is touched and fondled, the more he will respond. New babies do not understand speech, and their eyes do not focus well, so at first they will not learn by listening or looking. But even when they are very tiny, they learn by touching and by being touched.

The infant will know his mother's gentle caress before he is many days old. He will feel his daddy lift him in strong, caring hands. He will get to know the grandmother who tends him with confidence and love.

As the child grows, he will become a "lap baby" if he is lucky, and a warm hug, a squeeze, or a kiss will be positive input for him.

The art of touching does not come easily to some people, but it is never too late to discover the miracles it can produce. If you have not touched a child lately, what better time to do so than now, as a new family begins? Touch is a very important expression of love, and the very best grandchildren are the ones who are not afraid to love.

The new parents need not be left out either. The mother has done well. Why shouldn't she respond to an affectionate kiss? And why shouldn't the daddy enjoy a nice hug? Most people do.

———

Give advice only when you're asked.

Of course you are on the scene to help, but the help you give need not necessarily be verbalized. Remember that new parents are overwhelmed with advice. When it comes to babies, everyone is an expert. Everyone has either had a baby or been one. Neighbors, friends, doctors, and nurses all tell the uncertain new mother and the intimidated father what to do.

It is natural that every grandmother will have definite ideas on how to raise the baby, but remember that most young parents lack assurance at first. Like anyone in a new job, they are touchy about criticism. As they gain confidence, this sensitivity will pass. When they feel more comfortable asking for and receiving advice, you will not have to exercise your iron will quite so much. In the meantime, let the new parents know that you will be glad to tell them anything you can—anything they want to know that you do know—but that until they ask, you will hold your tongue.

When they do ask, give the most considered and considerate opinion you can, one that is untinged by criticism.

Phrases to be avoided at all costs are: "Well, if it were my baby . . ." and "Honey, I hate to find fault, but . . ." and "I was wondering when you'd notice that."

Don't be afraid to say that you don't know.

Part of the grandmother's "image" has to do with expertise. The grandmother likes to feel that she can hear a baby cry in the night and know instantly why he is crying. She also can change diapers in the dark, burp the baby more satisfactorily than the most experienced baby nurse, and deal with colic or diaper rash more easily than the best pediatrician.

Some grandmothers are indeed this efficient, but the best grandmothers, like the best friends, occasionally do not know all the answers and are not afraid to say so.

I think fondly of Alice, who called one day to ask a question about her eight-day-old son, Eric.

"I don't know," said Alice, "and my mom doesn't know either, and maybe you know."

Then Alice chuckled. "It was okay to hear Mom say she doesn't know. I used to think she was supermom and I could never measure up—you know, never be as good as she is. But if she doesn't know, it's okay for me not to know, isn't it?"

Alice's reaction was predictable. After a baby is born, new parents often feel a strong closeness to their own parents. They realize that it is not easy to be a parent, and they begin to appreciate the time, effort, and caring that they received from their mothers and fathers. They resolve to do as well for their own child, and if Grandmother has not overawed them with her perfection, they can face the task without being intimidated by it.

Make allowances for "baby blues."

———

49

A young mother can be terrified by the thought of being responsible for a tiny infant. At the same time, when the baby is new, she is trying to adjust to changes which have occurred and which are still occurring in her system. She may be exhausted from nights spent listening tensely for the baby to cry—and worrying when the baby doesn't cry.

The old wives used to say that a new mother was "not herself." Indeed, she may be as unlike herself as a changeling. She may be depressed and cranky, lashing out for no apparent reason. If Grandmother is nearby, she may be on the receiving end of the squall.

New mothers are not only easily irritated, they are also fiercely protective of their babies. There appears to be an almost biological instinct that dictates possessive behavior on the part of the mother. It made more sense when mankind lived in caves and the new mother had to protect her infant from marauding animals. Today we do not have that problem, but the instinct remains. It manifests itself in a need to feel in charge of the new family. It is important for the grandmother to let the mother be in control of her house and husband, and certainly of her child. Try to hold your tongue during this uncomfortable period and remember that your daughter does not really hate you or anyone else. Do not take it personally. This, too, will pass.

Usually the baby blues disappear as soon as the new mother gets a good night's sleep. They may return again if a light bulb burns out or a dish breaks. However, if the people around the mother are supportive, and the new baby is not too demanding, the depression and the fits of temper should be gone within a month.

———

The baby's temperament plays a big part in determining how well and how soon the new mother will adjust to her role and become her usual pleasant, well-mannered self. Some babies are placid and their mothers should be eternally grateful, but some babies are "screamers."

If the new baby is a screamer, the new mommy and daddy will be sure they are doing something wrong. They will be tired and on edge anyway, and the new mother will doubtless be on the verge of tears most of the time. Countless telephone calls will be made to the pediatrician.

Once you have ascertained that there really is nothing wrong—that the new arrival is just exercising his lungs and making his presence felt—the only thing you can do is assure the new parents that it is not their fault. The baby is crying because he needs to cry, and this fact has nothing to do with the way they changed his diaper or gave the bath.

Do not ever compare a fussy grandchild to your own "good" children.

Do not ever tell a young mother that her husband slept peacefully through the night when he was only three weeks old. Do not ever imply that the fretful baby must get his tendency to wail and weep from "the other side of the family."

First of all, having a "good" child is something for which you cannot take credit. It is as accidental as having a child with red hair or small feet. Secondly, the chances that your children were quite that "good" are small. Once a child is grown, we tend to forget the sleepless nights and the mornings filled with uproar, just as we tend to forget the labor pains. We only rejoice that a child was born into the world and — miracle of miracles — he or she finally grew up.

Neatness doesn't count.

If the young parents live in a house that is a bit untidy, they probably are more comfortable that way. Trying to bring perfect order to an extremely casual house could easily be construed as criticism. Besides, you were invited to share this important time with the new family because they love you — not because you are such a whiz with the vacuum cleaner. The new parents would much prefer that you give them the gift of your company and that you be relaxed and at ease with the new baby. That is what grandmothers are about. A sparkling, magazine-perfect home is not important. Loving and sharing are.

Give Daddy T L C too.

Before the birth, Daddy probably played a major role in getting ready for the baby. He may have done a lot of hand-holding and helping out with the chores. He probably went shopping or pushed a vacuum when his wife, tired and feeling fat, needed lots of emotional support and assistance.

Most expectant dads today attend weekly prenatal classes with their wives to prepare for their new responsibilities. Young fathers-to-be learn relaxation techniques so that at the time of labor they can help their wives. They are usually there in the delivery room, coaching and cheerleading, helping the mother to relax without a lot of medication.

After months of being almost an equal partner in the pregnancy, it can be quite a letdown for Daddy to come home and find that he is not as important in the daily routine as he once was. Mother and the baby are the center of attention. Flowers arrive, the telephone rings, people come to call, and Mother is told how beautiful she looks, and how delightful the baby is. Dad takes a backseat.

You can do a lot to make it better. First of all, do not ignore the young father. Make sure he knows that he is as important now as he was before the baby was born. Encourage him to help care for the baby. If he needs it, give moral support as he bathes or diapers.

Remember, no matter how many classes he has attended, the baby he is handling now is his very own. Young fathers may like to pretend that they are cool, but most share a common fear: they think they may hurt the baby if they do not handle him exactly right.

"I wish someone had told me ahead of time that babies don't break," said one man. "I was sure if I held my daughter close to me the way I wanted to, I'd snap her arm or a leg."

Assure the young father that the baby's little bones are still soft and almost unbreakable. The baby's skin will not tear if Daddy washes the baby's face. And Daddy's big hands and strong arms will make the baby feel very safe and secure.

When he is through with the bathing, diapering, or swaddling of the baby in a receiving blanket as they do in the hospital nursery, you might pamper Daddy and bring a pillow to prop his head. Or just give him an appreciative pat. He is tired too.

*Things get even better the
second time around.*

I have heard many grandparents say they could never love another grandchild as they did the first. I felt that way myself before my other five grandchildren arrived. But I have found that there is never a shortage of space in the human heart. It can always grow to encompass another love.

Grandma will be needed when the second child is brought home from the hospital. Perhaps her presence will be even more vital than it was with the first baby. If the mother is breast-feeding, she will have to devote much time to the new baby. Then a loving grandmother will give much-needed attention and assurance to the older child.

The household will be much more relaxed after the second baby. The parents will have more confidence and will feel easier about asking questions. They will be glad of the love you are giving to the older child, and so will you. Grandparents are supposed to have fun, and there are few things more fun than playing with a favorite grandchild and letting him know you think he's simply grand!

*As much as your heart can grow
heavy with rejection, remember that
little hearts break even easier.*

With family structures the way they are today, it might be that the newest arrival is your first grandchild. But it also may be that your daughter married a man who already had a four- or five-year-old from a previous marriage living with him.

Grandmas are grandmas, and there is nothing in the rule book that says that you cannot be as kind and loving an influence to your stepgrandchildren as you are to those who are your own flesh and blood. For example, if the older child does something special like starting the first day of school, and his parents want to share that time with you, stepgrandparents should show interest and excitement for the occasion. The time together helps strengthen the family structure and brings the family closer.

In today's changing world it is terribly important to accept stepgrandchildren in your life. And although you may not know it at first, you can have the same feelings for them as you do for your natural grandchildren. My husband and I certainly had the same feelings for the foster babies we cared for as we did for our own babies. It is hard to believe, but it is true. Once you have a child in your midst and you are caring for it and thinking about it and loving it, it makes all the sense in the world for your love to flow equally to all parties.

Living together means loving together.

Sometimes new grandmothers are concerned not because they live far away, as many extended families do, but because they live so near their children. This new grandmother can fear that the relationship with her grandchild will become humdrum and commonplace. This need not be the case.

To be honest, I cannot imagine any relationship between grandparent and grandchild becoming humdrum and commonplace. Grandchildren always are coming up with new and exciting things to talk about and explore, and every day brings forth something learned for the first time.

While grandparents always enjoy spending time with their grandchildren, sometimes this unique relationship can become overtaxed if the new parent takes it for granted, and this situation can occur if the extended family lives near one another. For this reason, my children and I never just "drop in" unannounced, nor do they assume that I will baby-sit all the time on last-minute notice. A phone call or a request beforehand, rather than an assumption, seems to make the relationship work more smoothly.

Even if you are accustomed to a very unstructured relationship now, after the baby arrives might be a good time to formalize things a bit, if just for a short time while the new mother gets used to her baby and his demands. When baby and mother are trying to nap, even the most well-intentioned, gift-laden grandma might not be greeted by more than a yawn and a less-than-enthusiastic smile.

While living close to your grandchildren may be the most emotionally rewarding part of aging, remember that sometimes you will want to say no when asked to baby-sit or to join your children and the baby for a particular occasion. As you are a grandma, so you also may be a wife, a working woman, a friend. You play many roles, and your children do too. And both sides will need to say no sometimes. Learn to do this without feeling guilty, and your relationship will be more honest and healthier as a result.

Today some grandparents live with their grandchildren so that the parents can work. This arrangement need not be a handicap to the grandmother who wants to establish a warm, special relationship with the grandchild either. There is much to be said for the family that has three generations living under one roof. With love and understanding, life in such a family can be richer for the children, the parents, and the grandparents.

Of course, the role of grandmother is slightly different if she is a part of the household. She becomes a sort of secondary mother, and usually shares responsibilities with the parents, helping with the decision-making and the discipline.

If this is to be the arrangement, guidelines should be carefully established at the very beginning. There should be a clear understanding about feeding schedules, the type of food the child will have, who will take the responsibility for marketing, laundry, toilet training, and other areas of child care. As the child grows older, he must learn what his responsibilities will be. The parents must always feel that the child will be cared for as they themselves would care for him, but they must understand, too, that Grandmother has beliefs and values. The relationships between the three generations will need to be reexamined at frequent intervals, and when problems come up, they should be aired immediately.

It is worth a great deal of effort to make an arrangement involving three generations successful. If child care is required and the grandparents are willing and able, it can be an excellent solution for working parents, and it can provide an ideal environment for the child.

❧

Long-Distance Grandparenting

*U*NLIKE many new grandparents, I was fortunate enough to have all six of my grandchildren born nearby, so I did not have to do any long-distance grandparenting while the children were in the newborn stages. However, when the eldest of the children was seven years old, she moved with her family to a small town more than one thousand miles from my home.

Of course, at the time their moving broke my heart, but I was consoled somewhat by the fact that my granddaughter was old enough to talk on the phone and to read the letters that I wrote to her.

Grandparenting a newborn from a long distance is a different and more difficult job. There is really not much you can do for the child (that he appreciates yet). He cannot answer you when his mom or dad holds the telephone receiver to his ear so he can hear Grandma's voice. As many photos as you have, until you see him, you never can really feel the radiance of his smile.

On the other hand, there is a lot you can do with the parents of the child to establish your role as a good and interested grandparent. One of your jobs is to help the parents and the grandchild to build memories, even in the earliest stages of the new family.

Photographs, of course, are wonderful, as are home movies. Even a three- or four-month-old baby can see Grandma and Grandpa on video and start relating to them. When the three actually meet for the first time, they will not be total strangers.

If you are a grandparent at a distance and you take a trip, drop a postcard to your grandchild. Or send an occasional letter not to Mommy or Daddy, but to young Johnny or Susie. Enclose a snapshot to show what you have been doing or where you have been. Or send a picture of Mommy or Daddy when they were small. It can be a keepsake that will find its way into the child's special collection of cherished possessions.

Another long-distance idea is to make video or cassette tapes of Grandma and Grandpa singing nursery rhymes or other songs. An audio tape of "Jack and Jill" sung by Grandma or Grandpa and played for baby in his crib is a good way for the child to get used to his grandparents' voices. Similarly, videotaping stories being read by Grandma or Grandpa will lock in the grandparents to the pleasures of their new roles as well as provide educational and entertaining stimuli for the baby.

One of the most wonderful things a grandparent can do is to visit with the grandchild when the baby is about three months old and to give the parents two or three days by themselves. No parent in this world could think of a greater gift, especially when the baby has begun to sleep through the night and the parents start to feel like a real couple again.

What could be nicer for a couple than to go away and have Grandma take care of their infant? It is a wonderful opportunity for everybody to contribute to a stronger family structure. Although taking care of a baby is not easy for grandparents, I can assure you that you will have a wonderful time, and when the few days have ended (and I do not think this is a good idea for more than a few days), you will know how great a gift you have given, and, hopefully, received.

Of course there will be marvelous times when your grandchild comes to visit at your house. Even if you can't splurge on expensive toys and fancy clothes, you can shop the garage sales for things that will appeal to the young- ster during the time you spend together. Even your overstuffed dresser or closet may be crammed with the perfect playthings for dress-up—old jewelry, handbags, ties, shoes and hats, which the grandchild will think are hilariously funny. Few grandchildren are ever bored with family photo albums or your collection of home movies.

One of the bottom drawers in my kitchen is filled with toys for when my grandchildren come to visit. There is nothing elaborate in the drawer—some measuring cups, spoons, a few little trucks, and a bunch of odds and ends that cost me next to nothing, things I found around the house that I thought the infants would enjoy.

The drawer is very low and lightweight, so the children could peek inside it from the time they were six months old, and they could always find some special thing in there. I have a tape measure that they can pull out, and when they push in the button on it, it flies back. That just tickles them to pieces. Other favorites are a twenty-nine-cent sponge shaped like a choo-choo train; and all the pieces to an old coffee percolator, which toddlers love to put together like a puzzle.

The bottom drawer existed for my own children, too, to entertain them when I was busy in the kitchen. And now, even the eldest of my grandchildren cannot help but open the drawer when she visits, just to know what's in there.

When your grandchildren visit your house, talk to the parents beforehand to remind them that it is your home, and your rules should apply. Of course, you have to be flexible with rules when little ones are around. Do not be surprised when, as soon as your house is shiny and clean for the visit, before you turn around, the children have put their tiny fingerprints on everything. At the time you might get frustrated, but when the visit is over and you look at those tiny fingerprints, they are wonderful reminders.

In terms of making the parents feel welcome, think of your best friend or husband's boss coming to visit, and set the stage in a manner suited to them. If you offer your family equal treatment, they, too, will feel very welcome. Have a sleeping area set up beforehand, with as much attention as you can pay to the baby's needs as well as the parents'. Perhaps place some flowers on a nightstand to help show that you have given some thought to what their time with you will be like.

There are also a couple of practical things that you can do to make life easier for the parents. Remember that they are going to be traveling with bushels of equipment, and it might be helpful if you can rent or borrow a car seat in advance so they do not have to bring theirs if they are flying. You can rent a bassinet or stroller too. Also I advise finding the name of a good pediatrician in your town. Heaven forbid, but if the child should get ill, you will have somebody to call who comes recommended.

There are lots of ways to babyproof your house, and once your grandchildren are crawling, it is important to secure your cabinets and to place harmful materials out of their reach. Also, put away your breakable treasures. There is nothing worse than having Aunt Sally's antique crystal bowl being broken the first day the children are there. So think about things you would feel more comfortable not having the children touch, and put them away before the new family arrives.

My personal preference is that when grandchildren come, the visit is limited to one child at a time. Not only does the time alone help each child to feel very special with his grandparents, it also gives the grandparents time to get to know that child as an individual with his own special needs, wishes, and dreams. You have to be with your grandchild to see what kind of person he is and how he feels about life. If it isn't possible to have your grandchildren visit singly, then do try to spend individual time with each child while they are there.

Recently, I spent several days in Mexico with my eldest grandchild, who is fifteen, and her younger brother, who is two. The eldest one rode horses on the beach while I took the baby in the ocean and built castles and pies for him in the sand. Spending time with the two children at totally different stages of development was a very special time for me, during which we all felt unique in our roles and with our relationships. On the last night of the visit I went to bed and found a note on my pillow. The note read, "I love you, Nana."

Of course, not all visits with grandchildren turn out perfectly, and sometimes the anticipation of the trip is very different from the trip itself. Often the grandparents are very excited about the visit, but when it actually begins, because there has not been a good relationship between the parents and the grandparents in the past, even daily routines can become a little bit strained.

My hope is that by starting to work things out during the pregnancy, by the time the baby comes, the relationship will have become a better one and such strains can be avoided.

Sometimes by the time the trip is over, you are more relieved than fulfilled. You might part a bit saddened because you failed to accomplish much. This feeling is all the more reason to set the stage well for these visits.

Even though your main reason for the visit is to see your new grandchild, it is a nice idea for you to spend an evening alone with the parents as well, maybe at dinner, with you offering to pay for a sitter. These moments give strength to the family as well as those you devote exclusively to the grandchildren. Even if you talk about the baby the whole time you are out, a "grown-up only" meal will give you an opportunity to reestablish your relationship and to acknowledge that the parents, too, are special people in your life.

*   *   *

While you may have saved up for a plane or train ticket to go to see your grandchild at his parents' home, it is very important also to keep in mind that few couples today have the extra money to entertain for even a week's time once you add up the cost of groceries and the extra use of household equipment. If your visit does pose a problem for the children financially, it might be a good idea to say in advance that you are coming to visit, and it would be your pleasure to send a little money to help pay for the additional expenses of groceries or gas in the car for sightseeing. Your visit should not be a financial burden on a couple that is strapped anyway once a baby is on the scene.

Some couples might feel hurt if you offer to pay for things, so if you do so and they refuse, then drop it. There are ways of sending gifts afterward, particularly if you have noticed a specific need in the young couple's household.

Probably the hardest part of long-distance grand-parenting for you will be your reluctance to accept the fact that you will not be on hand to watch your grand-child as he or she grows. But you need not be left in the dark either.

Even if the parents think you are being silly, encourage them to share the most minute of details about your grandchildren with you in letters, videos, and with photographs. Even the most trivial of events is certain to bring a smile to your face and help you recall days gone by when your own children lived through the same milestones.

One grandmother I know who has three or four children and seven or eight grandchildren has become so involved in learning about her grandchildren's everyday activities that she has become a clearinghouse for information among the extended family. Once a month, she gathers all the information from the entire family about what the children are doing—"Mary has a new tooth" or "Little John played his first soccer game"—and she writes a letter to the rest of the family summarizing everyone's news. Then she makes copies and sends the letter to all her children. The children do not have time to write these involved letters, and without them everyone would miss out on the news about their nieces, nephews, and cousins. At the same time, gathering the information and writing the letter makes the grandma feel involved and fulfilled, and her monthly contribution helps strengthen family ties.

Sharing news of your grandchild's development is especially rewarding for grandmothers because it brings back so many memories. I remember when my daughter's first tooth popped through. We were away from her grandparents, and I had to call one in California and one in New York to tell them about that little tooth. At the time my excitement was unbelievable. It was kind of a miracle to see that baby tooth in her smooth, pink gums.

When I spoke to my mother and mother-in-law, I wondered why they were so excited about the baby's first tooth. With all the teeth they had seen come through, I felt sure that to them the incident truly did not matter. But it did matter, I found out later when I became a grandmother, because my excitement at seeing it caused them to think back to when *their* babies had *their* first teeth and how excited they were.

Sharing those experiences on the phone and now on video . . . my goodness, can you imagine taking a picture of that first tooth as part of a video and sending it to the grandparents? The involvement can be so exciting because as a grandparent, you relive these things that you had forgotten.

Leaving the new family, or having them leave you, will not be easy. All grandmothers feel that the days pass too quickly, and with each day the attachment to that wonderful new person in the bassinet becomes stronger. Grandparents can look at the baby and see gestures that are strangely familiar. The baby is a further extension of a loved husband or wife.

You may want to stay indefinitely to watch the little personality unfold, but remember that you have your own life to go back to. If you go back to it at the time you and the new parents have agreed, you can look forward to years that will be enriched by the new child.

However, as you hold that tiny, sweet-smelling person in your arms to say good-bye, your heart does break. On the trip home, it might be hard to imagine not being close enough to share that baby's special milestones. The days that follow will be mingled with some sadness, but once you start showing off baby pictures, you will suddenly become part of a new peer group known as BAG ("bragging about grandchildren"). As you share your stories and pictures, your newest pride and joy becomes an everyday part of your life and makes the time between visits more manageable.

Gifts And Treasures

N E of the greatest joys of grandparenting is being able to give gifts to your grandchildren. When you have children of your own, you cannot always afford everything you want, and you end up buying practical things. Practical is always nice, but the real fun begins when, as a grandparent, you allow yourself to be a little bit frivolous.

What one-year-old needs a red car that he can pedal, complete with all the trappings of a real car including a make-believe telephone? Not too many one-year-olds can appreciate that. Yet I could not resist the one I saw in a catalogue. My grandson sat in it and smiled, and looked as though he loved it. It was a gift I really bought for me, because it gave me so much pleasure to give it to him and see his little face light up.

Of course, frivolous need not mean expensive if you live on a limited budget. It really means unnecessary, special gifts that stand out because they reflect the overwhelming joy in your heart rather than the practical dictates of your brain.

Making a white eyelet skirt for your grandchild's changing table could be called frivolous, especially after the first time he spits up all over it. But it is a special gift, and it makes you feel very proud to make and give it.

It is easy for grandparents to give frivolously when it comes to their grandchild's layette. So many grandmas I have heard about insist on crocheting the most adorable, satin-lined booties, even if their grandchild is born in July.

One grandpa I met in the waiting room recently had come to the hospital to see his daughter and his first grandchild, who had been born two months prematurely. The parents were not really prepared for the premature birth and did not even have any baby clothes to take the baby home in. So Grandpa volunteered to go to the nearest department store to do the shopping.

Wouldn't you know, he came back with the top-of-the-line layette . . . all in preemie size. And I haven't seen many men prouder than he was, carrying all those shopping bags to his daughter's hospital room.

———

With the exception of a case like this, once you have made or bought at least one unnecessary item, keep in mind that many parents will receive newborn clothes as gifts. These clothes really are cute, but the baby outgrows them so fast. If you can restrain yourself, it is more practical and may be appreciated by the parents more if you wait until the newborn gifts arrive, or until the children start outgrowing their baby things before you buy or make any clothing.

In the meantime, there are plenty of other gifts that new parents and babies will love.

- A crib mobile. Black and white ones are especially popular today because they are said to stimulate even the youngest infants.

- A cradle gym is an excellent toy for newborns. It is placed over the crib, and babies can kick it and grab for it for months until they can sit up.

- Rattles are good presents because at about three months, babies can grasp things for longer than a second or two, and they are fascinated by their ability to hold things in their hands. It is so cute to watch how startled they are when they shake their hands and the rattle makes noise.

- Stuffed animals, of course, are an old favorite. Be careful of eyes and other accessories that a baby can chew off.

- Tub toys are great fun, and do not cost much. Many tub toys can be made out of household items, too, such as funnels, sponges, and squirt bottles.

- Audio- and videotapes are among the newest newborn gifts, and they come in many voices and types. The most popular tapes among the young moms I know are those that feature intrauterine sounds, which are billed as the most comforting to the littlest tykes. Lullabies, rhymes, learning music, and mom-and-tot "exercise songs" also are well liked and can be appreciated by babies from the newborn stage onward.

Almost all the large toy companies note the ages that a toy is appropriate for on the package, so grandparents can be guided by the manufacturers' expertise. Also, grandparents should be aware of toy safety, which is another good reason to go with major toy companies. Their products are tested in-house and by independent groups.

There are a lot of toys on the market that I would not even think of buying my grandchildren simply because they wind up or have a battery, and offer no more stimulus for the child than to watch it. Toys that children can only watch are toys with which they get bored most quickly. I believe that children do much better with toys with which they can do something. Even a child as young as six months can sit on Mommy's or Daddy's lap and learn to build with blocks—how one block is put on top of the other and when the pile gets too high, it topples over. A very young child can understand that. I don't think there is a better toy in the whole world than a big bunch of blocks or Legos with which children can create their own things, rather than sit and watch a duck quack around the room.

When thinking about gifts, you may find that this is a good time also to plan in advance to purchase larger, more expensive items that the children may want or need

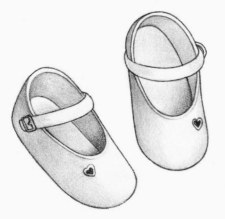

later on. Then you can budget your gifts and save up if you need to.

My son's godmother promised at my son's birth to buy all his shoes until he started school. So every time the baby needed shoes, we would buy them and send the receipt, and the godparents would reimburse us. It was very special for them because they knew that they were doing that for him and for us. I am sure that my son could not care less who paid for his shoes, but it meant so much to my husband and me that even though my son is now thirty years old, I still remember that his first shoes were bought by his godparents.

Another thing grandparents can do when a grandchild is born is to start a bank account for him. You can go out and spend a fortune on toys that are going to be ignored after a short period of time, and that is always fun to do (sometimes I think it is more fun for grandparents to *buy* the presents than for the children to receive them). But, if you can afford it, saving for the future is an equally thoughtful way to acknowledge the many milestones in your grandchildren's lives.

I started a bank account for my first grandchild, and to this day, although I do send her a little gift on her birthday, most of the gift is money that I give her as a check for her bank account. If grandparents can afford it, a bank account is a good way to build funds for college.

I do not think a child is ever too young to receive his own books. Building a library for your grandchild can have a very special meaning for years to come. I know one grandfather who, along with buying the very first book, built a shelf for the books to go on. And the very first books and the very last one the grandparents had sent were all on this shelf that Grandpa had built. The very first books were the clothbound ones for the children to chew on, and they were pretty worn. As the books became a little more sophisticated, they were signed by the grandparents with dates on them and words of love that I am sure will go on for years and years to remind the child not only how much he loved the stories, but also to remember that Grandma and Grandpa sent the book to them, and what they were thinking about when they did.

Another type of book that I highly recommend is the homemade kind. My husband's parents wrote a journal to my first daughter when she was born, describing their lives in the early part of the century. They passed along the journal to me, and I added to it as well, making notes about my daughter's childhood. Now the journal has been passed along once again to my daughter in the hopes that she will continue to write in it and extend the family history for the next generation.

———

Books of photographs and memorabilia also make wonderful and unique gifts. One woman I know assembles photographs of her grandchildren and arranges them in a scrapbook each year for their birthday. Along with the photos, she writes in the book annual "letters to my grandchild" describing the events and milestones that the children reached during that year.

Not one to make scrapbooks myself, I prefer to make photo collages of specific visits or trips with my grandchildren to fit in eight-by-ten or twelve-by-fourteen-inch frames. Over the years I have made several of these "photo essays" for my grandchildren to hang on their walls.

I don't think anything gives grandparents more pleasure than to visit a toy or clothing store and buy something special for their grandchild. That is going to be a pleasure all your life. But you can get started in a no-win situation with your grandchild if you always arrive with a gift in hand. You do not want your grandchild, as he gets older, to expect that every time he sees Grandma or Grandpa, a present is coming. Then, instead of looking forward to seeing you, the child learns to look forward to seeing what you have brought him.

Infants, of course, will not know who brought them gifts. But as your grandchildren get older, it might be advisable to arrive without a gift once in a while, and then perhaps sometime during your visit take them to a store and buy one.

Often another way to avoid the Santa Claus dilemma and to have a little fun with gift-giving is to send your gifts for no occasion. I almost always get a call after doing this. And that is special too. You need not wait for a birthday to come along if you see something cute that you think a particular grandchild would like. Just send it.

In this day of rampant consumerism, you might be intimidated into believing that you will be seen as a less-than-perfect grandparent if you cannot afford to give your grandchild a special present for every occasion and during every visit. With all the important roles that grandmas and grandpas play in teaching their grandchildren about respect and love and finding their way in the world, nothing could be further from the truth. If you love your grandchild and give to him from your heart, he will return that love and respect regardless of the size of your pocketbook.

One of my favorite stories about my oldest grandchild and her total indifference to the cost of her toys begins with the tradition that all of you will experience someday of having your grandchild sit on your lap. Grandchildren seem to love to sit on their grandparents' laps, perhaps, as mine says, because "Grandma, you're so softier. When I'm on Mommy's lap, her bones hurt me."

Grandchildren also love the way Grandma smells. I have been using the same type of perfume for years, and one time when the children were leaving, my eldest grandchild, who loved to sit on my lap, said, "I don't want to leave because I will miss the way Grandma smells."

On hearing that innocent plea, I quickly ran into the bedroom for a piece of cloth, stuffed cotton for a head, and tied a bow around the neck to make a doll. Then I sprayed the doll with my perfume, and gave it to my granddaughter.

She is fifteen years old now, and to this day every time she comes to visit, she brings the doll to get a couple of squirts of my perfume for it. Sometimes when I talk to her on the phone, she reminds me that it has been too long since our last visit because her doll has lost all of its smell. The reminder of her love and how much she misses me is a subtle but powerful one.

Your grandchild will not care if you live on a very restricted budget, believe me. Grandma is warm, cozy, and loving, and she always has time. To the child, that is what is important. Even if you do not live near your grandchild—even if you make your home in some distant part of the country—you can be warm, close, and loving. You can set aside special times for sharing with your grandchild. And that is the greatest gift of all.

SIX

❧

The Best
Is Yet to Come

*N*O matter how many communes anybody invents," said anthropologist Margaret Mead, "the family always creeps back."

Life-styles have changed since we had our own families. However, grandparents have not become obsolete. They are needed now more than ever. In today's nuclear family, grandparents can provide stability, continuity, and tradition. And, of course, once you are a grandparent, you will be a grandparent forever.

You will continue to have a place in the family even after the new mother has fully recovered her strength and even after the child is grown.

Most grandparents want above all to be close to their children and their grandchildren. It is not always easy for us to accept a new life-style, however. We may find it difficult to maintain a loving, nonjudgmental attitude when we see our children doing things we would not have considered at their age—or at any age! But if we are going to be generous in our loving, we must be tolerant of different values and different styles. The prayer for serenity might have been written for today's grandparents:

God grant me the serenity to accept the things I cannot change, the courage to change the things I can, and the wisdom to know the difference.

Even if we think something can be changed, it is important to be practical as well as wise and to put up a fight only for those principles that we feel are absolutely vital. Although they may reject our values, our children do not want us to reject them. They need our support and love. And as time goes by, we will find that there is no generation gap between ourselves and our grandchildren. We understand each other perfectly.

After your grandchild's infancy is over, the true delights of being a grandparent unfold. You will find yourself sharing good times with the child. You will begin to play again, and you will discover a new sense of adventure.

You do not have to discipline your grandchild; your special times with him are for fun. Mother and Dad occasionally may have to be stern, but you can just enjoy the child's company.

Grandchildren are for spoiling, just a bit, and it is a rare child indeed who does not appreciate being spoiled now and then. Grandparents are people who play with children whether they are busy or not. They also cuddle children who have mumps, and bake them cookies when they are well. As I wrote in the beginning of this book, who could ask for a more noble mission in life?

Without question, your time is the most precious gift you can give your grandchild. For the littlest grandchild, being rocked by Grandma is a special experience, and he will respond to the strength and security found in Grandma's arms.

As the grandchildren grow, the things that grandparents can share with them become more varied and more fun. Cookies and cakes taste twice as good when they are made with the help of the grandchild. A walk is a high adventure and not just a way to get from here to there. On the way to the supermarket with Grandma, the child can see butterflies and flowers. Perhaps he can watch a fire engine roar past, or he and Grandpa can pause to watch a steamroller clanking along. Parents have busy schedules and heavy responsibilities. They may not have time for butterflies, fire engines, and steamrollers, but grandparents often do. They are, to quote the children, "the people who play whether they are busy or not."

The cookies and the cakes and the expeditions to see fire engines and to explore woods and parks are delights to both grandparent and child. Even more delightful is the storytelling. Grandmother is the one who can tell the children about Mother or Dad. Grandpa remembers what the parents were like when they were little and what they did. And from a child's point of view, grandparents are people who have lived a long, long time—ages and ages—and who know what it was like in the "olden days."

Grandparents will be wise if they anchor their grandchildren in reality and make sure they realize that Grandpa and Grandma never crossed the Great Plains in a covered wagon, churned butter, or did lessons by the light of a tallow candle. However, grandparents' stories of their own growing years can expand a child's awareness of the continuity of a family and all of life. When a child understands where his grandparents stand in relation to Mommy and Daddy, he will better understand his own place in the family.

Grandparents' stories do not help only the grandchild. They help the grandparents themselves. They give us an opportunity to go back to our own childhoods. We remember the stories our grandparents told us, and for the child, the world becomes a larger place. Because they have listened to their grandparents' tales, their memories can stretch back for several generations. Through our grandchildren, our hopes go forward and we look into the future when the child will be an adult and perhaps a parent himself.

In addition to sharing the family stories, you can participate in wonderful adventures of make-believe with your grandchild. You may want to reread some of the books that you loved as a child, or that you read to your own children. Or browse the bookstores for new stories.

My grandchildren loved *The Little Engine That Could*. When they were a bit older, we read *Charlotte's Web* to them. One of my all-time favorites is Margery Williams's *The Velveteen Rabbit*. This is a story about a stuffed toy who wants very much to be real and who learns from a shabby old toy horse how one goes about this.

"Real isn't how you are made," says the horse. "When a child loves you for a long, long time, not just to play with you, but really loves you, then you become real . . ."

Children understand this lesson because they have not yet become calculating or cunning. Reality is simple and open; it is loving and being loved, and grandparents can be the beneficiaries of this innocence.

Sometimes it is the grandparents who need care and not the grandchild. We all develop some infirmities as we age, and the presence of a grandparent who isn't always jolly—or even comfortable—can give the child a chance to understand that age exists as well as youth. If children are to be complete people, they need to understand and care for older people. They need to see the entire spectrum of life.

Sometimes the generations need to be apart. Grandparents face the prospect of grandparenting with different degrees of dedication. I would be greatly amiss if I blithely assumed that all grandparents will enjoy caring for their grandchildren. Perhaps you will not, at least when the babies are very young. You should not feel guilty if this is the case. You may enjoy your grandchildren more when they are older.

The nice part about grandchildren is that you can enter their lives whenever you feel comfortable.

But you may not want to wait. You may be eager to be a grandmother, doing all the grandmotherly things. You may have perfected your recipe for cookies, knit several dozen booties, and rehearsed all your favorite lullabies. You may then discover that the new family has decided to go it alone.

One grandmother I know said, "I did everything right. What did I do wrong?"

Probably she did nothing wrong. The young parents did not really mean to reject her; it is unfortunate that she felt hurt and disappointed. She should not have taken the decision personally.

Some young couples are not comfortable taking help at first. They may be insecure in their new roles, and they may need time before they can welcome a grandparent as a part of their new family.

Grandparents have to make sacrifices, but they can gain so many rewards. If you are reading this either before or immediately after your grandchild is born, it may seem that you will be giving a great deal. The first weeks of a child's life are difficult for the family. They are a time of adjustment, of working through complex new relationships. You may grow weary of showing sensitivity, understanding, discretion, and kindness. "Is this really worth the trouble?" you may wonder. *It is!*

As the child grows, you will feel that you have helped create a solid foundation for the new family. You can look forward to a happy future with your child and your grandchild. You have started upon the wonderful, exhilarating time of being a grandparent. I like to think that grandparents have a certain measure of invincibility. They get better with age, never worse. As the toy horse explained to the velveteen rabbit, "Generally by the time you are real most of your hair has been loved off, your eyes drop out, and you get loose at the joints and very shabby. But these things don't matter at all, because once you are real you can't be ugly, except to people who don't understand."

Grandparents are indeed real. And are they ever ugly? Surely not, for the children do understand.

Dear Friend,

It has been great fun writing this book, and I am excited to think that as you read it, you will be starting on your new life as a grandparent.

My personal experience as a grandmother has been very rewarding. Life is not always perfect, even for grandparents, but it is an ongoing, three-generation-growing experience. And there is no doubt that the very best part comes when you feel two soft little arms around your neck, and you hear the words "I love you, Grandma!"